Editor Chester Fisher
Assistant Editor Dale Gunthorp
Design Patrick Frean
Picture Research Ed Harriman
Production Philip Hughes
Illustrations John Shackell; Ron Hayward Associates; John Mousdale; Marilyn Day; Tony Simmonds; Tony Payne; Jim Antoniou
Maps Matthews and Taylor Associates
Special Consultant Dr. K. Tofallis, Director of the Greek Institute

First published 1974
Reprinted 1978, 1980, 1982, 1984
Macdonald & Co (Publishers) Ltd
Maxwell House, Worship Street,
London EC2A 2EN
A member of BPCC plc

© Macdonald Educational Ltd. 1974

ISBN 0 356 04854 3 (cased edition)
ISBN 0 356 06517 0 (limp edition)

Printed and bound in Great Britain by
Purnell & Sons (Book Production) Ltd
Member of the BPCC Group,
Paulton, Bristol

Greece

the land and its people

Jim Antoniou

Macdonald Educational

Contents

The cradle of the West

The first Greeks

The Greek civilization began during the New Stone Age, at about 4000 B.C., and reached mainland Greece in the early Bronze Age, about 2800 B.C. It started at Knossos on the island of Crete, which until about 1400 B.C. was the centre of the brilliant Minoan civilization. This Minoan culture gradually spread over the Aegean world.

From about 1600 B.C., certain places on the Greek mainland began to rival Crete as centres of civilization. The chief of these centres which succeeded Knossos was Mycenae. Recently a young British architect, Michael Ventris, broke down the code of a mysterious script found on Mycenaean and certain Cretan clay tablets, and established that the language was an archaic form of Greek.

Homer's *Iliad* is set in a late stage of the Mycenaean Age. Agamemnon, King of Mycenae, led the united Achaeans to Troy very early in the 12th century B.C. (traditionally believed to be 1194 B.C.). By the end of the 12th century B.C., the Mycenaean Age came to an end.

In turn, the Dorians came down from the north into central Greece. This invasion began a dark age which lasted some 300 years, after which Classical Greece of the Hellenes began to emerge.

The Greek idea of life

Older civilizations of the Near East were often extremely efficient in practical matters, but remained intellectually barren. The Greeks were not very numerous. Neither were they very powerful. Although they were not very well organized, they had a totally real conception of what human life was about.

The classical Greeks divided humanity into Hellenes and barbarians. The Greek word *barbaros* did not mean "barbarian" in the modern sense. It meant that people who did not speak Greek made noises like "bar-bar". Anyone who did not speak Greek was considered a barbarian—meaning that he did not think as a Greek.

▲ Wall paintings in the Palace of Knossos, Crete, date from 2000 B.C. The Minoan civilization of Crete attained a high degree of craftsmanship.

▼ The Parthenon on the Acropolis built from 448 to 438 B.C. Temples stood as monuments dedicated to gods and as attempts to achieve perfection.

The distribution of peoples in Ancient Greece

MACEDONIA

THESSALY

AEGEAN SEA

Gulf of Corinth

ATTICA

ARCADIA
PELOPONNESUS

IONION SEA

SEA OF CRETE

CRETE

- Ionians
- Dorians
- Aeolians
- North Dorians
- Arcadians

▲ Greek writing developed over many centuries. The Romans based their writing on Classical Greek. The Church based its teaching on sacred books written in Greek during the first centuries A.D. The Russian language today uses similar letters to Greek.

▲ The Lion Gate at Mycenae (built about 1400 B.C.) forms an impressive entrance to the royal citadel. This ancient city in the Peloponnese was believed to be the home of the Greek king Agamemnon, who appears in Homer's *Iliad*.

▶ Greek sculptors in the 5th century B.C. managed to solve technical problems and introduced movement and grace into their works of art. Bronze and marble were the main materials used, This bronze statue of Poseidon, the God of the sea, was found in 1928.

Mountains, plains and islands

▼ Greece has two contrasting parts: the mountainous mainland peninsula at the tip of the Balkans and the numerous islands, of which some 166 are inhabited today.

A rugged land

Greece lies on the crossroads of three continents. Even including the islands, Greece is a small country (132,562 sq. km.: 107,078 sq. km. of mainland and 25,484 sq. km. of islands). Greece has never been able to support more than a few million inhabitants. The present population of Greece is 9,360,000 which is about the same as Greater London. Approximately 52 per cent of the Greek population is urban and 48 per cent rural.

Greece is a land of hard limestone mountains, the highest being Mount Olympus (2,917 metres; 6,570 ft.), deep valleys and a jagged coastline 15,020 km. (945 miles) long. It is cut by the narrow divide of the Corinth Canal (originally conceived by Nero and carried out during the last century between 1882 and 1893). It makes the

◀ Kavalla, with its Byzantine fortifications, is a bustling port and commercial centre on the main highway from Thessaloniki to Istanbul. It is the main outlet for tobacco grown in Eastern Macedonia and Thrace. Before the Turkish occupation it was named Christopolis in honour of the Apostle Paul who first set foot on European soil there in 50 A.D.

Peloponnese, a large peninsula shaped like an oak leaf, theoretically an island. To the east, lie a scattering of islands. To the west there is a further group of seven islands. The whole pattern is completed by the long rampart of Crete to the south.

Each district or island has its own history, folklore and customs which have contributed to the culture of the country as a whole. Many dialects are still spoken and traditional costumes are worn on festive occasions. Parts of Greece are quite well known for certain specialities, such as wine, cheese, fruit, olive oil, or honey.

The Greek people have very strong ties with the rural areas of their origin. On some festive occasions, particularly Easter, people from the towns and cities tend to go back to their villages and spend time with friends and relations.

▲ Athens, the capital of Greece, is a city which grew rapidly after World War II. It is a modern, bustling metropolis. Syntagma Square (seen here) is the hub of Athens and reflects the cosmopolitan atmosphere of hotels, banks and airline offices.

▲ Greece is mostly a mountainous country, with few plains, and the soil to a large extent is unfit for cultivation. Rainfall is irregular and high temperatures in summer further lower agricultural yields. Sheep and goats have been the mainstay of livestock breeding in Greece for centuries. Each day they are led out to remote and barren landscapes.

Some Greek national costumes

Central Greece	Skiros	Macedonia	Salamis
Ipiros-Souli	Lefkás	Skiros	Corinth
Corfu	Ipiros	Thessaly	Thrace

The Greek influence

Ancient Greece

Greece has played an enormous part in the history of Western civilization. The major achievement of ancient Greece lies in the unshakeable belief in the worth of the individual person.

Greek law, based on popular consent, aimed at improving conditions for all citizens (though no woman, foreigner or slave could become a citizen). Laws could only be changed by being referred to the citizens for their approval.

The Greeks developed and made extensive use of a wonderfully subtle and expressive language. They also used tragedy to express the ·darker and more difficult relations between gods and men. Ancient Greek literature is as alive and relevant today as it was when it was first written.

Observation and experiment

The Greeks became the founders of science by way of philosophy (literally meaning "love of knowledge"). The nature of the physical world excited their curiosity and led them to make spectacular scientific theories. Greek science also saw the need for observation and experiment. Scientific medicine began under the great physician Hippocrates of Kos. He collected data from which deductions could be drawn. Mathematical terms were used to express technical knowledge. The Greeks were the first true historians and founded schools of history which are still relevant today. Accounts of past events gradually changed from legend to fact.

Over 2,000 years later, the modern Greeks find themselves and their national role diminished in world importance, but they are deeply aware of their national heritage and strive to produce works of art of simplicity and charm. In the economic life of the modern world, Greek ships sail all the world's seas, and Greeks do business in all the world's commercial centres.

▲ Alexander the Great (356-323 B.C.) was admired for his great conquests. Many powerful military leaders tried to emulate him. The detail above is from the remnants of a Pompeii mosaic.

▼ Euclid (330-260 B.C.) lived in the days of Ptolemy and was the most important mathematician of Hellenistic times. His "Elements of Geometry" are still used as a basis for teaching mathematics today.

Some Greek gifts to the world

▲ Greek architectural principles are apparent in many public and educational buildings all over the world.

▲ Many mathematical formulas, theorems and principles taught in schools today were first discovered in Greece.

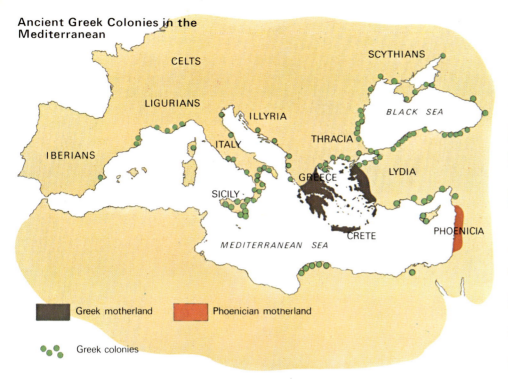

Ancient Greek Colonies in the Mediterranean

CELTS

SCYTHIANS

LIGURIANS

ILLYRIA

IBERIANS

ITALY

BLACK SEA

THRACIA

GREECE

LYDIA

SICILY

CRETE

MEDITERRANEAN SEA

PHOENICIA

■ Greek motherland   ■ Phoenician motherland

● Greek colonies

▼ Greek workers at a Volkswagen factory in West Germany. Thousands have become guest workers in foreign lands. In 1976, 500,000 Greeks worked in West Germany and sent valuable foreign currency back home.

▲ During the 8th and 7th centuries B.C. the Greeks spread all over the Mediterranean and colonised its shores. Greek culture influenced all these colonies in ancient times. The Romans later expanded the area of Graeco-Roman influence.

▼ Greece is one of the world's major shipping nations. Greek-owned ships include huge oil tankers, bulk-cargo carriers and many passenger ships. Piraeus, which is the largest port in Greece, has many shipyards in which large and small ships are built.

▲ Greek citizens discussed important issues, then decided policy by voting. Modern democracy is based on the same principles.

GREEK FOOD

▲ Emigration, particularly to the U.S.A., has played an important role in introducing Greek ideas to other countries.

Family life

Outdoor living

Some villages, especially in the poor and mountainous regions of North Greece are very remote, with few facilities. Families live in dwellings which consist of one or two rooms and a small courtyard. In the large towns and cities people usually live in flats. Residential streets are often lined with rows of apartment blocks.

The mild climate allows outdoor living for most of the year. Outdoor space can be a courtyard, a garden, a verandah, a balcony, the pavement outside the front door, the street or an open air café in the town square. Because of the wide use of outdoor space, dwellings need only be quite small. The living room is mostly reserved for formal occasions and guests.

Although Greek women spend much time cooking, the kitchen is usually quite small with only simple facilities. In rural areas, very often the cooking is partly done in the open air. Sunday dinner is often prepared at home and taken to be cooked in the local bread oven. This provides more cooking space and the chance to chat with friends.

A close family life

Outside the large centres, in particular, Greeks are brought up in an atmosphere in which women are regarded as inferior. This view includes wives but not mothers. The Greek man's mother is sacred, and he will not allow anyone to show her disrespect. Old people usually live with and are taken care of by their children. Particularly outside the large towns, a girl needs a dowry, and in most cases her brothers may not marry until she is safely taken care of. The dowry may be in the form of property or money. Girls spend much time in their village preparing a trousseau.

A Greek wife does not feel she has really done her duty to her husband until she has borne him a son. Children are more under the control of their parents and family relatives have more say in each others' affairs than is usually tolerated in North European families.

◀ Traditionally, Greece has been an agricultural country and peasants have led a harsh life over the centuries. In the villages streets are narrow with simple buildings, whitewashed as protection from the sun.

▲ Surburban houses in Athens. They are usually built of concrete with brick or block infilling, plastered and painted in bright colours. Concrete reinforcements are often left exposed for further buildings.

▲ The way of life in poor and remote villages is very hard, with few facilities available to the family. Women work for the menfolk and have to use old fashioned methods.

An average family budget

- 30% Food & beverages
- 20% Housing, fuel & light
- 15% Services & other goods
- 10% Clothing & shoes
- 10% Transport & communication
- 8% Education & health
- 7% Durable household goods

A typical daily timetable

6.30
8.00
2.30
3.30–5.00
5.30
8.30
8.30
10.00
11.00
1.00

▲ The family spends much time together. Children are more under the control of their parents than is usually tolerated in North European families. This family comes from Crete. Even the oldest girl is completely under her parent's authority.

Leisure and pleasure

Dancing and discussion

The Greeks are a high spirited and jovial people, rarely missing an opportunity to enjoy themselves. This is reflected in their night-life establishments, where local singers are accompanied with live music played on "bouzoukia"—an instrument not unlike a mandolin. Very often people become so enthusiastic that they break dozens of plates on the floor. In the course of the evening customers get up and perform popular Greek dances, either in groups or alone. The *Sirtaki* is one of the most popular Greek dances, although it dates back only to the end of World War II. Variations are danced all over Greece.

The café ("Cafenion") is the forum of the Greek village. Traditional Greek coffee is served in tiny cups and is accompanied by a glass of cold water. Greek men spend much of their leisure time in such cafés, discussing many topics and playing a popular game called *tavli*.

Outdoor pastimes

Watching football is a national pastime. Next to politics, football is the most discussed subject in Greece. Football league matches are played on Sunday afternoon. International matches or Greek cup finals are played on Wednesdays.

During the hot summer the Greeks take to the sea—either to swim and sunbathe, or to sail, water ski, fish, or just play on the beach. Families try to hire accommodation by the sea for the whole summer season.

Some leisure activities

▲ Greeks love to argue. They shout at each other, but calm down quickly. Often the issue is who is to be blamed.

▲ Many Greeks are keen on small game shooting and the sport is controlled by strict game protection laws.

▼ Greeks enjoy a night out. Customers get up and dance together. Others become enthusiastic and throw plates on the dance floor.

A day on Greek television

Channel I
13.45 Programme of traditional songs and dances
14.05 Cyprus: news and events
14.20 Cartoons
14.45 News
15.00 Current affairs programme
15.15 Close down

18.00 Programme on conservation of nature
18.30 Lassie
19.00 In the Service of Man (profile on the fire brigade)
19.15 Main news
19.30 Greece—the Golden Land
19.45 Women's discussion programme
20.00 The Waltons
20.55 Poetry and Harmony
21.30 Main news
21.55 Gunsmoke (Western)
22.50 This Week (current affairs)
23.05 The Sons of Cain (film)
News and close down

Channel II
13.45 Same programmes as
15.15 on Channel I
17.55 Mackoe family (series)
19.00 Children's world
19.30 News
19.50 Greece and the Sea (documentary)
20.10 The Greek people (documentary)
20.25 Road without Return
20.45 Motoring programme
21.00 Viva Katerina (comedy)
21.30 News and weather
21.50 Our neighbourhood (local culture)
22.20 Police file (film)
Late night news and close down

▲ Greeks like to read their newspapers carefully and then discuss local and international issues amongst themselves. Individual newspapers and magazines have to cater for a wide cross-section of Greek society.

▼ Greek villagers are very sociable and the men like to sit in the open air cafes usually found in the square. They occupy the best places from which to observe action and participate if they feel inclined.

▲ Aliki Vouyouklaki is a leading popular film star. Her films are made for Greeks, so she is little known outside. Many Greeks follow her career in newspapers and magazines. She usually co-stars with Dimitris Papamihail.

▲ Nana Mouskouri is a Greek singer of international fame. She sings with a group of musicians called "The Athenians". She performs in many countries and is well known on British television where she often has her own programme of Greek songs.

A Sporting people

▼ The ancient Greeks made the Olympic Games part of their religion. While the Games were on, lasting five days, all warfare between Greeks had to cease. Only Greeks were allowed to enter the stadium at Olympia. The Games were revived by Baron Pierre de Coubertin and took place in Athens in 1896.

Home of the Olympic Games

Greece is the country which gave birth to the Olympic Games. The traditional date of the first Olympic Games is 776 B.C. In modern times an attempt has been made to revive the same spirit and ideals of the Olympic Games. The first modern games were held in Athens in 1896. The Olympic torch which lights up the Olympic Games is lit from the ancient site of Olympia.

In Ancient Greece, youths were very enthusiastic about athletics. Today track and field atheletics are still very popular. A large sports ground centre has been established in Athens at Agios Cosmas. It includes football fields, basketball and volley-ball grounds, tennis courts, running tracks and a hostel.

The most popular sport in Greece today is football. Teams have ancient names such as "Olympiakos" (Olympian team) and "Panathenaikos" (after the goddess Athena). The largest grounds are in Athens and Piraeus.

There are many other sports which are popular with Greeks. Amateur basketball is fast gaining popularity. The season starts in October and ends in May. Volley-ball is now gaining nationwide interest. Similarly, swimming contests are held on almost every weekend. Water skiing is also popular and there are many ski schools at coastal areas.

Sports out in the open

The ideal months for sailing in Greek waters are April to October, and even November. From December to March 60 per cent of all days are sunny, and many yachtsmen sail their craft all the year round.

Game shooting is permitted in all regions according to strict preservation laws. During the season there are quail, turtle dove, partridge, woodcock, thrush, waterfowl, hare, wild boar.

▼ A football match between Greece and England. Football is the most popular sport in Greece. When an important match is on, the streets of Athens are almost empty until the game is over. People who cannot go to the match follow it on the radio or television.

▲ The largest skiing centre in Greece is at Metsovo. From January to mid-March there is permanent snow above 1,500 m. in Greece.

◄ The Acropolis Rally is 3,100 km. long and is considered as one of the most important events of the European Championship.

▼ Cricket is played on the island of Corfu where matches are arranged between the two local and other visiting teams from Britain.

▲ The largest football grounds in Athens are the Panathenaikos (25,000 seats), AEK (35,000 seats) and Karaiskaki (45,000 seats).

A great desire for education

▼ A group of schoolchildren in a village. Greek parents encourage their children to work hard. Pupils attending State schools wear simple blue and white uniforms, representing the Greek flag.

Public and private schools

Children start school at the age of six. In addition to public schools, there are also many private schools for all grades. Some private schools also teach a foreign language such as English, French or German. Private schools provide their own transport. School buses of all types and sizes criss-cross the main cities to get children to and from school. Public school children usually wear a simple uniform with blue and white colours (like the Greek flag), but do not wear caps.

Class sizes vary widely and overcrowding is a growing problem. In large cities schools are on dual sessions, with some children coming only in the morning and others only in the afternoon. In public primary schools there are 34 pupils to each teacher. In private primary schools there are 27 pupils per teacher. Many pupils and students pay for private tuition to supplement their lessons. Special tuition is also given at private learning centres called *frontistiria*.

The Greek school system

► Primary education is compulsory. Secondary schools fall into two categories: the *Gymnasio* for 12-15 year olds and the *Lykeio* for 16-18 year olds. Secondary school students must pass examinations to obtain their certificate. Those who do not gain entrance to a University may go to Higher Technical Education Centres.

Kindergarten 3-6 years

Primary school 6-12 years

Postgraduate study

University 18 years and onwards

Technical college and higher education

Secondary school 12–18 years

For some a private tutor

Higher education

Public schools are built and maintained by the government. The government's source of revenue for schools comes from income tax. The government also supplies textbooks to pupils free of charge. Supplementary books and materials are expensive purchases for the students who wish to study further.

The first university of Athens was housed in a building which is still standing and is located in the old part of Athens. Today there are universities at Yianina, Patras, Thessaloníki and Athens. At Athens there is also the Polytechnic (National Technical University). Competition to get into these institutions is very high and entrance examinations are stiff. Many young people also go abroad to study.

Higher Technical Education centres have also been established at Thessaloníki, Larisa, Athens, Patras and Iráklion. Throughout the education system, relations between pupil or student and teacher are kept very formal.

▲ Pupil-teacher relations are kept formal, and lessons are academic. Teachers receive their training in three-year academies.

◄ Boys like to play games and some facilities are provided for their use in the playground. Basketball and volleyball are popular games.

▼ The University of Athens, built in 1837 by the Bavarian architect Christian von Hansen, is the best neo-Classical building in Athens. In Athens, there is also the Polytechnic (National Technical University) and there are universities at Patras, Thessaloniki and Yannina. Competition to get in is high.

A religious nation

A social event

The Orthodox Church is administered by seven patriarchs. Today the Greek Orthodox Church plays a dominant role in society. It is necessary to be a member of the Church to advance to high positions in Greek society.

A person must be christened. Papers, identity cards, or any kind of licence cannot be obtained before one is registered with the church. A provincial bishop is a very influential person. He is usually chairman of almost every social institution in his See. Churchgoing is a social as well as a religious event. In many parts of the country, especially on some of the islands, there are almost as many churches and chapels to be seen in the village as there are houses.

In a village wedding the banns of matrimony are signified by paper crowns joined by a ribbon. Some village weddings take about 5 days.

The importance of religion

The Orthodox Christian Church is the official religion in Greece and originated during the Byzantine period, when Christianity developed two centres: one at Byzantium, one in Rome. Greece then formed part of the Byzantine Empire. During the Turkish occupation of Greece, priests played a leading role in preserving the Orthodox faith and the Greek language. The monks and village priests held secret classes at night for young Greeks.

The major church service takes place on Sunday morning and can last three hours. Churchgoers take their places according to a rigid system. Women stand on the left, the men on the right. The children gather around a dais near the front. The churchgoers go round the church, lighting candles, and kissing icons. A screen divides the priest from the people. There is little opportunity for the congregation to participate in the service.

▲ Many miracle cures have been attributed to St. Dyonisios, patron saint of the island of Zákinthos. On his annual feast day his body is borne in procession through the streets.

▶ Inside a Greek Orthodox Church the nave is separated from the sanctuary by a screen called "iconostasis". It is sculptured in marble or timber, painted and gilded. This church is at Anoja.

▲ The Byzantine Monastery of St. John the Theologian (who was exiled to the then remote and lonely island of Patmos) was built in the 11th century. Much of the land on Patmos is still owned by the Church.

▼ At the Monastery of Arcadi, 500 men and women died during the Cretan revolution against the Turks in 1866, when the abbot Gabriel set fire to powder kegs, also killing many of the enemy, rather than surrender.

▲ All over Greece, along the roads, small shrines dedicated to particular saints can be seen. Some commemorate an event that took place there, or they may be dedicated to a church or monastery close by.

▲ In Greek society, the priest has an influential role and is a very respected member of the community.

Custom and superstition

▲ The principal religious festival on the island of Corfu is that of St. Spyridon, patron saint of Corfu seamen. His embalmed remains were brought to Corfu in 1489 and encased in a golden casket.

A respect for custom

The Greek language is rich in sayings and superstitions. Each region in Greece has special celebrations, sayings and customs. Customs have a profound effect on the way of life of the people—particularly in rural communities.

Young girls are always expected to look attractive in order to appeal as potential brides. In rural communities the rules of behaviour for single girls and the rules of courtship are strict and closely enforced by conscientious families. Parents, brothers as well as members of the extended family watch over her reputation and behaviour. Most parents would rather have sons than daughters.

Responsibilities of married women include all household duties: childrearing and working with their husbands in the fields. In Manoklissia, a village in northern Greece, women take over the role of giving orders once a year, by lounging in cafes, or doing men's work, while their menfolk do all the household chores.

A superstitious people

At Goumenitsa the *kourban* is celebrated at a wayside chapel. Here the traditional sacrifice of a calf takes place, with a simple banquet and folk dances.

There is usually a taboo against women accompanying fishermen on their boats, and so only the men of the family go in search of fish. The reason fisherfolk give, is that women, in their ignorance of fishing superstitions, may step on the nets, thereby violating the inherent symbol of the cross formed so many times by the criss-crossing sections of thread. This could cause bad luck and jeopardise the catch.

Older people in some villages hate and fear local gypsies. They believe it was the gypsies that made the nails for the cross. Old people also believe that blackbirds nest around the house of the non-orthodox Greek.

A Greek who has a lot of bad luck believes that someone has put the "evil-eye" on him (i.e. has cursed him). Charms showing an eye are often carried as a protection against evil spirits.

▲ On May Day people collect flowers from the surrounding countryside and make wreathes which they hang on their doors or balconies.

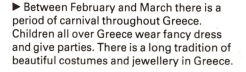

▶ Between February and March there is a period of carnival throughout Greece. Children all over Greece wear fancy dress and give parties. There is a long tradition of beautiful costumes and jewellery in Greece.

▲ Many poor people try to make a living by selling lottery tickets. Greeks buy these in the hope that they will win large sums of money and solve all their financial problems.

Some Greek customs

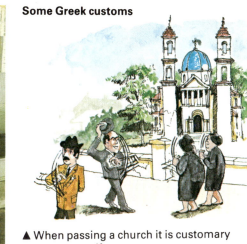

▲ When passing a church it is customary to cross oneself.

▲ Greeks pass the time playing with strings of beads called "Comboloy".

▲ Greeks like to dress up and stroll in the streets on Sunday.

▲ The Greek philosophy of driving is to rely on the other person's brakes.

▲ In rural communities the rules of behaviour are strict and closely enforced. Old people are respected and have a lot of say in the morals of the family. Responsibilities of married women include all household duties, and working with their husbands in the fields.

Shops and shopping

A demand for good service

The Greeks always go for the best food. The Greek housewife buys simple fresh food in season. Markets may be held weekly, or permanently. In Athens, the centre of commercial activity is the area around Athenas Street. Here can be found the vegetable market, the meat and fish markets. In small villages, the local grocery shop is also the butcher shop and the local cafe. In Greece, bread and cakes are mostly made and sold on the premises.

In the suburbs people prefer to go to a shop where they know the man who runs it. This way they expect a better service. Supermarkets are spreading fast in the urban centres, but usually they are of small scale, compared to other European countries.

The flea market

In shops other than food stores, Greeks often expect to bargain for the price of items. The fashionable Kolonaki area has many small top quality shops for men's and women's clothes. The flea market, close to Monastiraki Square, takes place every Sunday morning, where large and colourful selections of second hand items are sold.

In most towns, at most street corners, along pavements on main roads there are also small rectangular kiosks selling many items including cigarettes and newspapers. However, most of them are like tiny supermarkets, open almost round the clock and packed with tourist guide books, postcards, sun glasses, films, shoe-laces and watch-straps. The majority also have a telephone for public use.

▲ People prefer to shop where they know the man who runs it. This way they can expect a better service.

◄ Greeks like to peck during the day. They buy rings of bread with seeds on them, which they eat with cheese.

▼ Another common item sold on street corners during the winter is hot sweet corn, which is grilled on a slow charcoal grill.

Greek money

▲ Greek money is measured in drachmes and lepta. The biggest note is 1,000 drachmes and the smallest coin is 5 lepta. There are about 120 drachmes to £1.

▲ In Athens, the centre of commercial activity is around Athenas Street. Here can be found the vegetable market, the meat and fish markets. This is a stall in the fish market.

▼ Every region in Greece produces its own type of wine or spirit. Here the shopkeeper is decanting *retsina,* the traditional Greek resinated wine.

Eating the Greek way

A typical day's meals

Breakfast:
Greek coffee, and perhaps a slice of bread

Mid-morning snack:
Tomato and cheese with bread

Lunch:
Vegetable dish or salad, with bread and beer

Supper:
Fish or meat dish, with vegetables, salad, bread, and beer

Food with character

The Greeks like to eat well and, after centuries of experiment, have introduced a specific character to their food. Greek cooking has borrowed from Western European as well as Oriental cooking. The main ingredients used are olive oil, fresh tomatoes and lemon.

Breakfast is simply Greek coffee (a strong thick mixture consisting of fine ground coffee, sugar and water), similar to Turkish coffee. Luncheon in Greece is, as a rule, served about 2 p.m. and lasts for an hour or so. Greeks have their evening meal comparatively late, around 10 p.m., and it can last well into the night. A Greek meal is usually preceded by *ouzo* (aniseed aperitif). It is distilled from crushed grape stems. The traditional Greek wine is *retsina* (i.e. resinated, to keep better). The main dish may also be served with fresh salad. There are also many cheeses with regional variations, the most famous being *feta*, made from goats milk.

Greece is very much a country where one can visit unfashionable country inns miles off the beaten track. Restaurants close to the sea serve a wide variety of sea foods: lobster, squid, octopus, red mullet and shellfish.

Make yourself a Greek meal

TZATZIKI
½ pint of yoghurt
½ cucumber, peeled and cubed
1 clove garlic, finely sliced
salt and pepper

Mix all the ingredients together and serve very cold.

MOUSSAKA
2 lb. aubergines
1 lb. minced meat
3 tablespoons grated onion
3-4 ripe tomatoes
1 tablespoon chopped parsley
¼ teaspoon cinnamon
2 oz. butter
2 oz. grated cheese (kefalotiri is best if you can get it)
¾ pint white sauce
2 eggs
salt and pepper
olive oil for frying
bay leaves

Slice the aubergines and leave them to soak for an hour. Then allow to drain in a colander for at least 30 minutes. Fry a few slices at a time until they are nicely browned on both sides. Melt butter in another pan and saute the meat, onions, chopped tomatoes and bay leaves. Add parsley, spices and seasoning and moisten with water. Cook for 20 minutes and then remove from the heat and allow to

GREEK SALAD
1 large onion, sliced
3 firm tomatoes
½ cucumber
black olives
1 green pepper
olive oil and vinegar dressing

Toss all the ingredients in a bowl. Mix the dressing well and pour over the salad.

A selection of Greek appetizers

Taramosalata — fish roe paté

Tzatziki — cucumber and yoghurt

Olives

▲ The Greeks like to eat delicious titbits called "mezethes": dolmades (vine leaves filled with minced meat and rice); *Keftethes* (fried meat balls) *taramosalata* (fish roe paté); *tzatziki* (yoghurt and cucumber salad); olives.

Dolmades — stuffed vine leaves

Keftethes — meat balls

cool. Butter a large roasting pan and fill with alternate layers of aubergine and minced meat, sprinkling each layer with a little grated cheese. Add the eggs, well beaten, to the white sauce and pour over each layer. Sprinkle the remaining cheese on the top and bake in a hot oven until the top is golden brown.

Chopped pieces of feta cheese can be added as an optional extra.

▲ At meal time the family eats together. The mild climate of Greece allows the family to eat out in the open air during most part of the year.

▼ Fruit is plentiful: apricots, peaches, honey melon, water melons, grapes and figs. There are also pastries such as *baklavas* and *kataifi*.

Melon

Peach

Grapes

Figs

Baklavas — honey and almond pastry

Kataifi — almonds and honey in shredded pastry

A glorious artistic past

The three architectural orders

▲ Doric (6th century B.C.). Doric columns developed from the heavy wooden beams used in the pre-classical buildings.

▲ Ionic (5th century B.C.). Later architects added the scroll decorations to the capital and delicate fluting of the column.

▲ Corinthian (4th century B.C.). Decoration of the capital became more elaborate and the columns still more slender under this third architectural order.

The many Greek arts

The modern Greeks are deeply aware of their national heritage in all their works of art, and strive to produce works of simplicity and charm. Every summer in the preserved ancient theatres of Epidaurus, Dodoni, Eretria, Philippi, the ancient Greek plays of Aeschylus, Sophocles, Euripides and Aristophanes are performed.

At Knossos in Crete, the bright colours of frescoes in the Palace of Minos are still visible. Monasteries contain examples of frescoes, or mosaics of Byzantine art.

Homer's *Iliad* and *Odyssey* were the foundation for the ancient Greek's education. Since that time they have played a significant part in the development of Western literatures. One of the most well known of modern Greek writers is Nicos Kazantzakis who has written many books, including "Zorba the Greek".

Music and sculpture

The ancient Greeks discovered the relationship between mathematics and musical notes. This made it possible to write and study music. Two famous composers of Greek popular music are Manos Hadjidakis (who wrote the music for the film "Never on Sunday") and Mikis Theodorakis (who wrote the music for the film "Zorba the Greek"). Maria Callas, who died in 1977, was a world-famous Greek opera singer.

Dances have been performed for centuries in Greece. From fragments of vases found, it is believed that many traditional dances date back to ancient times. From the eighth century B.C. to the present day, the folk dances of Crete are said to have the same basic characteristics.

◀ This famous bronze statue of the charioteer and parts of the four horses and reins were found at Delphi in 1896. It is one of the finest of classical bronzes by Polyzalos created in 476 B.C.

▲ Mistra, near Sparta in Peloponnese, was an independent principality for almost two centuries. Its churches and wall paintings are among the greatest achievements of the Greek Byzantine times. These frescoes in the Periuleptus church belong to the 14th century. They depict scenes from the life of Christ.

▶ Attempts have been made to bring back the ancient drama to the Greek theatre. As a result, ancient tragedies and comedies in the original setting are being performed again. Artists such as Katina Paxinou, Anna Synodinou and the internationally known Greek director Karolos Koun have contributed to this revival of Greek drama.

▼ Mikis Theodorakis, composer and folk-singer, achieved international fame through his protest songs about conditions in Greece after the army coup of 1967.

▲ The most original feature of the Erechtheum on the Acropolis is the six statues of the Karyatids, or young maidens. They stand in place of columns, 2 metres high. One of the Karyatids is at the British Museum.

An ancient innovation

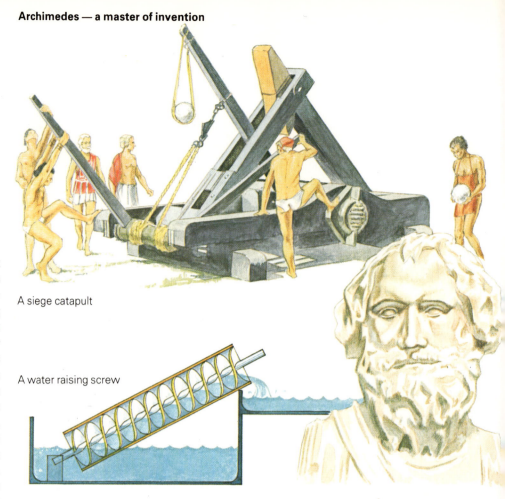

A siege catapult

A water raising screw

Understanding the universe

Greek speculation, based on logic, about the origin and nature of the universe resulted in many inventions and discoveries. This was achieved by building up a body of scientific truth, based on observation and experiment. In all their discoveries the Greeks had a sense of the wholeness of things. They took the widest view and saw things as parts of an organic whole. The Greeks believed that the universe itself was a logical whole and, despite appearances, was simple in its structure. Mathematics was the most characteristic of all Greek discoveries and the one that excited them most. Pythagoras discovered the mathematical basis of the musical concords. Similarly, Euclid was the most important mathematician of Hellenistic times. His work "Elements of Geometry" is still used as a basis for mathematics as taught in schools today. The word "geometry" is Greek for land measuring.

Early discoveries

Thales of Miletus, a practical man, devised ways of measuring the distance of ships at sea, based on his knowledge of geometry. He was also an astronomer who predicted that during the year 585 A.D., the sun would be totally eclipsed.

Aristarchos of Samos established that the earth rotates on its axis and revolves around the sun. He also established that the earth is the shape of a globe.

Anaximander made the first map. Nearchos, Alexander the Great's admiral from Crete, sailed through the Indian Ocean. Pytheas of Marseille set out on a long journey of exploration in the Atlantic and is said to have sailed to England. Eratosthenes drew up a map of the known world from the information obtained by these explorers.

▲ Archimedes was a physicist and engineer as well as a mathematician. He studied in Alexandria but worked in Syracuse. He invented various engines of war and used these to help his adopted city when it was besieged by the Romans. He discovered the so-called Archimedes principle about the specific gravity of bodies, and first showed the significance of the principle of leverage. He was the greatest physicist of antiquity.

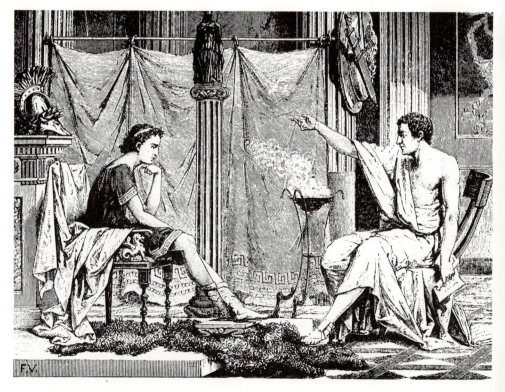

Pythagoras — a master mathematician

▲ Pythagoras (c. 582 – c. 507 B.C.) was born on the island of Samos. Discoveries believed to be his are the multiplication table, the decimal system and the Pythagorean theorem.

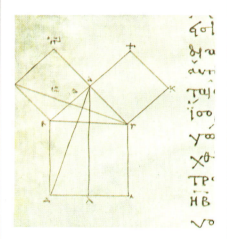

▲ The Pythagorean theorem, first expounded over 2,000 years ago, proves that in a right-angled triangle the square on the long side is equal to the sum of the squares on the two shorter sides. The Babylonians had discovered this earlier, but Pythagoras was the first to prove it. To this day builders depend on it, to lay out rooms as perfect rectangles.

◄ Aristotle, like his pupil Alexander the Great, was born in Macedonia. He tried to initiate Alexander in the ancient heroic tradition and attributed much importance to the teaching of Homer's Iliad and Odyssey. In 368 B.C. Aristotle became a student at Plato's Academy in Athens. He had the ability to isolate problems. Aristotle created two branches of philosophy: logic and metaphysics.

Ptolemy's universe

▲ Ptolemy, guided by the muse of astronomy, measuring the altitudes of the moon with a quadrant. He did this with surprising accuracy in the second century B.C. His ideas were accepted until the 16th century A.D.

▼ A map of the universe, based on Ptolemy's astronomy. Ptolemy understood the principle of the rotation of heavenly bodies, but mistakenly placed the earth at the centre of the solar system.

Craftsmanship and industry

▲ Grapes have been known in Greece for more than 3,500 years. They were the favourite fruit of ancient Greece. Crete produces a grape called "rozaki" shown being harvested here.

▼ The art of pottery painting is a tradition handed down from ancient times. The Greeks today produce many fine ceramics, inspired by ancient designs. Tourism has boosted the ceramics industry.

The prime place of tobacco

Greece is an agricultural country. Farm production accounts for most of the country's exports. These are mainly tobacco, cotton, citrus fruit, raisins, fresh fruit and vegetables. Other products include honey, wines, pistachio nuts and olives.

Of the cultivated land in Greece, 3.5 per cent is for tobacco, providing work for a million growers (i.e. 20 per cent of the peasant population). Tobacco plants are small and plucking takes up much time. Traditionally, plots are small and are worked by a whole peasant family. Some 80 per cent of the yearly output is destined for abroad and the rest is for the domestic market.

Efforts have also been made to industrialize the country. One of the most important industries is textiles. At present Greece manufactures enough cloth for the home market. Other important industries are oil refineries, nickel production, and ship building. There is also a flourishing cement industry.

Tourism is a major industry, providing employment and valuable foreign currency.

Regional handicrafts

Greek handicrafts follow ancient traditions. Skills are handed down from generation to generation, and fine work is done in bronze, marble, wood, wool, silk, metal, silver, gold and clay. Different regions have their own crafts: hand-woven skirts, lace, embroidery, copper work, beautiful silverware, jewellery and copies of ancient and Byzantine articles. Greek handicraft products sell well in towns and cities.

The people of Arachova specialize in colourful patterned handwoven woollen blankets, and large bags called *tagoria*. The region of Ioannina produces silverware and ornaments. Rhodes produces gold and silver ornaments of its own style, as well as pottery. Mykonos is famous for its weaving and embroidery. Metsovo is famous for wood carving. Kalamata produces fine silks, and Kastoria is world renowned for fur-trimming.

◄ The sea is an important source of food in Greece, and Greeks are skilled in small and large boat building. Here the hull of a fishing boat is being built. Greece is one of the most important shipping nations in the world.

▲ Patterns of weaving have been handed down for centuries, different ones in each region. Colourful hand-woven blankets and large bags called "tagoria" are made in these patterns. This woman, spinning cotton is from the village of Kato Figaria in Arcadia.

Some Greek products

Textile-making

Oil-refining

Merchant-shipping

Ship-building

Fishing and canning

Donkeys to airliners

A mobile nation

The main focal points of the country's transport services are Athens (for land and air transport services) and Piraeus (for sea transport). Another important focal point is Thessaloniki, serving the north.

The total number of motor vehicles on the roads in Greece is 414,736. The Greek road network covers 39,000 km. (24,000 miles) of which 14,500 km. (9,000 miles) are asphalt paved.

The port of Piraeus is the starting point and terminal for all Greek coastal shipping services. The main islands of Greece are linked together by frequent steamship and car ferry services.

The national airline, Olympic Airways, operates all domestic air routes, with regular air services to the large urban centres and many islands.

Improving communications

New locomotives and railway coaches have been procured and all passenger trains are diesel operated. Only freight trains still have steam locomotives. The Greek State Railway has plans to improve fast train services. Soon it will be possible to travel by train from Athens to Thessaloniki in 3.5 hours.

Road traffic regulations in Greece are the same as those in force elsewhere in Europe. The Greeks drive on the right. In the large towns there are many one way street networks.

Bus fares are cheap, and vary according to distance. The centre of Athens is also served by yellow electric trolleys. There are also 9,000 taxis in the Greater Athens Area and a further 5,000 in Thessaloniki, the second city of Greece.

▼ In spite of technological progress, donkeys are still a familiar sight and are used as a regular means of personal mobility in the rural areas. There are some 559,000 donkeys and mules in Greece today.

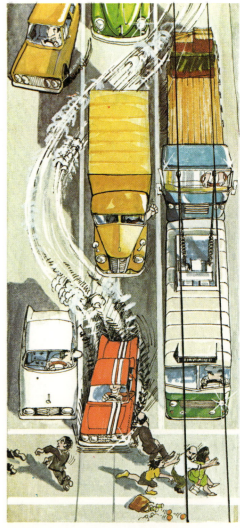

▲ Driving in Greece is a hazardous experience. The Greek driver wants to show how clever he is at cutting in, overtaking, beating the lights and finally screeching his brakes. People on foot are seen as a constant nuisance, rarely given way to by Greek drivers.

Olympic — the airline of Greece

▼ Olympic Airways is the national airline of Greece. It is the only Greek airline and has achieved an international reputation, with regular flights to most parts of the world. Within Greece, all commercial aeroplanes, helicopters and aerotaxis belong to Olympic Airways.

Olympic airlines Symbol

An air taxi—Alouette II

Boeing 747—200B

▲ Blue and white buses and yellow trolley buses operate in major towns. An additional service is the electric train operating between Piraeus and Kiphissia, via Athens, which it crosses underground.

▶ The Corinth Canal was constructed during 1882-93, based on the plan by Virlet d'Aoust. It is 6,300 metres (4 miles) long, 21 metres (69 feet) wide at the bottom. It makes Peloponnese theoretically an island.

▼ Sea transport is a major service in Greece. Daily services link larger islands to the mainland. Motor boats carry passengers from these islands to smaller ones. The network is linked to the mainland through Piraeus.

Athens
city of the
sacred rock

An ancient city

The Acropolis (156 metres, or 512 feet, above sea level) in Athens has been inhabited since about 3000 B.C. but the city did not develop until sometime around 1300 B.C. when Theseus united the townships of Attica. The Acropolis became the spiritual centre of Athens, crowned by the Parthenon, the home of the city's goddess Athena, while the Agora below was the centre of political, social and commercial life.

Athens is vividly described in a text of the third century B.C. "The city is dry and ill-supplied with water. The streets are nothing but miserable old lanes, the houses mean with few better ones among them. On seeing the town for the first time the stranger would hardly believe that this is Athens of which he has heard so much."

The planning of Athens

During the Turkish occupation, the Acropolis became a village with the Parthenon converted into a Mosque. Greeks were not allowed on the Acropolis. After the War of Independence, the Greek Government commissioned plans for the future development of the city as the capital of Greece. The plan was based on wide streets and squares structured on a triangle of three main streets.

Plaka is the oldest inhabited area of Athens and contains much of the city's history. Syntagma (Constitution) Square has been an open space since ancient times, when Theophrastos (371-297 B.C.), Aristotle's successor, had his private house and garden there. Aristotle's gymnasium is thought to have stood in the same area as the national gardens today. The rocky peak of Lycabettus is one of the most prominent features of the Athenian landscape, second only to the Acropolis.

▲ Reconstruction of Athens in the time of St. Paul (50 A.D.). The Acropolis was the spiritual centre of Athens, crowned by the Parthenon. The large temple to the left was dedicated to Olympian Zeus in Roman times.

◄ Plaka, literally meaning slab, is the oldest continuously inhabited area of Athens situated on the slopes of the Acropolis. Along narrow streets, many restaurants and shops are a great attraction to tourists.

▼ Athens remains a young city. People from all over Greece migrate to Athens for employment and a more exciting life. The shops, cultural activities and lively city atmosphere are as attractive to Greeks as to tourists.

Things to see in Athens

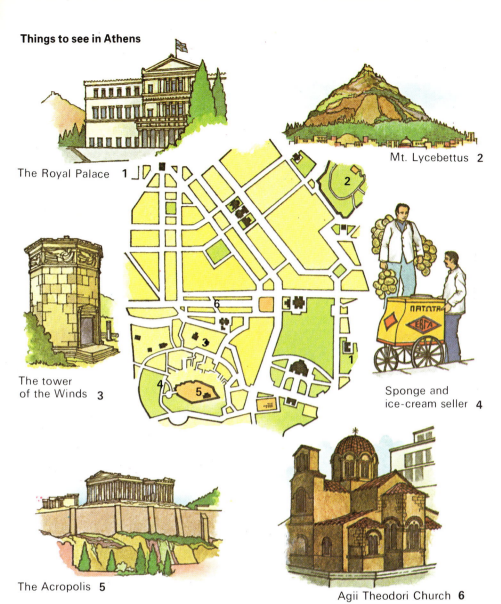

The Royal Palace **1**

Mt. Lycebettus **2**

The tower of the Winds **3**

Sponge and ice-cream seller **4**

The Acropolis **5**

Agii Theodori Church **6**

▲ Below the Parliament Building is the grave of the Unknown Soldier, guarded by soldiers called *evzones* dressed in national costume. The changing of the guards ceremony is a picturesque attraction for tourists. They also guard the Royal Palace even though Greece is no longer a monarchy.

Some Athenian pastimes

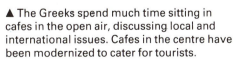

▲ The national gardens in the centre of Athens are a favourite place to escape the heat and noise.

▲ The Greeks spend much time sitting in cafes in the open air, discussing local and international issues. Cafes in the centre have been modernized to cater for tourists.

▶ During the summer Greeks try to spend as much time on the beaches close to Athens as they can. At lunchtime buses are full of workers going to the beaches.

The islands jewels of Greece

The charm of the islands

Among the unique features of Greece are her islands. Each one has its own identity, local colour, its own setting and history. Many of them are untouched by modern technology and in consequence have kept their character and charm. There are 166 inhabited islands and 1,259 deserted ones. Some of the latter have been bought by wealthy people.

The Cyclades are a group of islands in the Aegean Sea. Kea, Kythnos, Seriphos, Kimolos, Siphnos, Milos, Folegandros, Sikinos, Ios, Santorini, Anafi, Amorgos, Naxos, Paros, Antiparos, Mykonos, Delos, Syros, Tinos, Andros, are all islands in the Cyclades. These islands lie close together forming a circle with Delos at the centre—hence the name Cyclades. Delos is the mythical birthplace of the god Apollo and is the most sacred island of ancient Greece—no mortal could be born or die there.

Another group of islands are the Saronic Islands, that is Aegina, Poros, Spetsai and Hydra. In the northeast Aegean Sea there is a cluster of large and rich islands: Limnos, Lesbos, Samos, Ikaria and Chios. The people of Chios claim that Homer was born there.

The Ionian Islands, with their rich culture have been the crossroads between mainland Greece and Western Europe for centuries. There are seven islands in this group: Corfu, Paxi, Lefkas, Kefalonia, Ithaki, Zakinthos and Kithira.

In the south east part of the Aegean Sea are another group of islands known as the Dodecanese (meaning "twelve islands", though there are actually thirteen). Rhodes, rich in history, is the largest and easternmost of the Dodecanese.

The group of islands known as Sporades ("scattered isles") is situated in a semi-circle around the Cyclades—to the south, the east and north. Crete, with its long history of civilization is the largest Greek island and the fifth largest in the Mediterranean.

▶ Patmos is where St. John the Theologian lived and wrote the Book of Revelations in a sacred cave. The historic eleventh century monastery provides fine views of the town below.

▲ Delos, the birthplace of god Apollo and goddess Artemis, was sacred to the ancient Greeks. The lions were a gift from the people of Naxos in the 7th century B.C.

▲ Mykonos is one of the most fashionable islands for visitors. It has dazzling white houses, narrow twisting streets and some 360 churches. Its windmills and churches such as Paraportiani are regular subjects for painters.

▶ Crete is Greece's largest island. It is the centre of the ancient Minoan civilization. At Knossos are the excavations begun by Sir Arthur Evans in 1900 and his reconstruction of the palace of King Minos. There are many charming sea towns in Crete, like Aghios Nikolaos on the Gulf of Mirabello.

▼ Men from Kalimnos are renowned as sponge divers. Every year during late spring, they depart in the fleet of boats for five months for North Africa, off the Barbary Coast, to carry out their dangerous task.

Lesvos

Chios

Samos

Patmos

morgos   Kalimnos
          Kos

Dodecanese

Rhodes

Carpathos

▲ Rhodes was seized in 1306 from the Genoese by the Knights of St. John of Jerusalem, who settled there. The old town is dominated by the Palace of the Grand Masters, with tall, crenellated towers.

▲ Rooftops in Lindos, Rhodes. Lindos was a major city in classical times, and remained a centre during the Middle Ages when the Knights of St. John built the lovely white church of Our Lady of Lindos. Many of these houses date from the Turkish period.

▼ The Convent of Vlachernae in the foreground and "Mouse Island", Corfu, behind it. According to legend, "Mouse Island" is the ship of Odysseus, turned to stone after his return from Troy. The Convent is a favourite subject of painters.

The City State birthplace of democracy

The right to speak

The Greek word for city state is *Polis*. In the ancient polis, citizens considered it their duty to take part in all the affairs of the polis—or "political" affairs. The state was small, and Aristotle believed that each citizen should be able to know all the others by sight.

The Greeks (ancient and modern) like to spend their leisure time strolling and talking in the town and square. Ancient Greeks thought life was a barren affair for anyone who lived more than a day's walk from the centre of the polis.

This small state was governed by an Assembly. All citizens were members of the Assembly. It met at least once a month and discussed all state business. Any citizen could speak and anyone could propose new laws or action by the state. This was the beginning of democracy.

War and peace

Ancient Greeks had time to participate in the running of the state because their lives and needs were very simple. Women (who had no political rights) and slaves did much of the work that had to be done. The Greek citizen got up at dawn, shook out the blanket in which he had slept and draped it elegantly around himself as a suit. He had a beard and therefore did not need to shave. In five minutes he was ready to face the world.

So much was the *Polis* the community of citizens, that in times of war the citizen had to find his own equipment: the man rich enough to own a house served in the cavalry—on his own horse. While he was in service the *Polis* paid for its keep. The moderately well-to-do served in the heavy infantry (*hoplites*), providing his own armour. The poor who could provide nothing but themselves, served as auxiliaries or rowed in the fleet. Slaves never served in either army or navy, except in a moment of great danger. At such times they were invited to enlist with the promise of freedom and full, civil (not political) rights.

▲ The Royal Grave Circle at Mycenae. This early city state (1600-1150 B.C.) was very rich and powerful. It carried on a large trade throughout the Mediterranean.

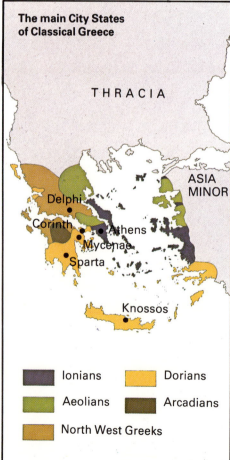

The main City States of Classical Greece

THRACIA

ASIA MINOR

Delphi
Corinth
Athens
Mycenae
Sparta

Knossos

Ionians — Dorians
Aeolians — Arcadians
North West Greeks

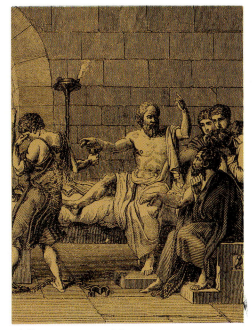

▲ Socrates was a philosopher whose teachings provoked the rage of many Athenians. He was committed to trial and sentenced to death in 399 B.C. He chose to die by drinking hemlock.

▶ A reconstruction of the market place of ancient Athens. Under Pericles, every citizen of Athens had the right to vote and could be elected to any office.

▼ In 491 B.C. the powerful Persian emperor sent a fleet to conquer Greece. The Athenian army met and fought them at Marathon. Though the Greeks had fewer men, their superior armour and experience gained them victory.

Some Greek gods

Zeus

Hera

Apollo

Aphrodite

Ares

The struggle for freedom

▲ Mahmoud II, Ottoman Sultan of Turkey during the Greek fight for independence.

Turkish domination

Greece has been conquered by Romans, Goths, and Franks. The most complete occupation was by the Turks; it began in the fifteenth century and lasted for nearly 400 years.

In 1814 the *Philiki Etairia* (Society of Friends) was founded and became the rallying point for all Greek patriots. Its charter clearly laid down its recruiting methods and aims. One of its most famous members was Theodoros Kolokotronis. Under his leadership Tripolis, the Turkish administrative capital of Peloponnese, was captured in 1821. From there, the revolution spread to other parts of Greece.

The siege of Missolongi

The town of Missolongi rebelled against the Turks and was twice besieged. Lord Byron, the poet and adventurer, died there, deeply disappointed, for at that time the Greeks were endlessly squabbling among themselves. During this terrible siege, the Greek patriots regained their reputation. Eleven thousand Turkish soldiers surrounded the town, defended by 4,000 Greeks.

Death in battle or from disease or starvation claimed 2,000 of them, but the town held out for one year. Then, on 26 April 1826, a desperate plan was put into action. The surviving soldiers burst through the Turkish lines. When the Turks entered Missolongi, the non-combatants there destroyed it, killing the conquerors and themselves. This heroic act put new courage into the Greeks, and all over Europe people responded to the Greek call for freedom.

Then help came from abroad. In 1827 the fleets of Britain, France and Russia destroyed the Turkish navy in the Bay of Navarino. In 1829, Sultan Mahmoud, Emperor of the Turks, brought the fighting to an end by conceding independence.

Independent Greece

By the Convention of London in 1832, Greece became an independent kingdom. The monarch had to come from one of the royal families of the three big powers. A Bavarian prince called Othon was chosen. Though Othon reigned for 30 years, Greece was troubled by political unrest which has continued to the present day.

▲ The siege of Missolongi, 1825-6. On 26 April 1826 the attacking Turks broke through and entered the town. But the 3,000 women and children there were prepared; they blew up the town, the conquerors, and themselves.

▶ In 1827 the combined fleets of Britain, France, and Russia destroyed the Turkish navy in the Bay of Navarino, annihilating Turkish naval power. The three Great Powers and Sultan Mahmoud signed a treaty in 1829.

▲ George Gordon, Lord Byron, one of England's great poets, gave moral as well as financial support to the Greek struggle for Independence. He died of malaria in Missolongi in 1824.

▲ A young Bavarian prince called Othon was chosen as the first king of independent Greece. His father appointed a regency council to rule till Othon was older, much to the annoyance of Greek politicians. King Othon was deposed in 1862.

▲ Demetrios Bulgaris headed the provisional government which deposed King Othon. Othon, who had no heir, was forced to leave the country. Greece had no monarch for a year until a suitable candidate had been selected. Seventeen-year old Prince William of Denmark came to the throne as George I of the Hellenes.

War and civil strife

Invasion by Italy

Italy, under Mussolini, urged the Greeks not to offer any resistance to the Italian army which marched into Greece on October 28, 1940. The Greeks, however, had been conquered too often, and decided to resist. At that time, Greece was the first country to fight back against the Fascists. The Greek attempt at self-defence greatly impressed the free world. Each year, October 28 is still celebrated with military parades all over Greece.

The Greeks were poorly equipped to withstand the Italian army. Their numbers were smaller, their weapons out of date. They were not equipped for prolonged warfare in winter on remote mountains.

Germany intervened on the side of the Italians, and the Greek army was defeated. By the end of April 1941 the whole of Greece, with the exception of Crete, had been taken by the Germans. Crete was later captured by the Germans after a long battle. The Greeks fought the Nazis with two underground armies (one was communist controlled). Over 350,000 Greeks died. Some were executed, others died in concentration camps, in armed clashes during the occupation, or finally from starvation.

Greece was liberated by the Allied Forces in October, 1944.

A savage civil war

A full scale civil war erupted after the liberation, when the communists tried to take over the country. More people were killed during this period than by Germans and Italians in the war. By the end of 1947 some 800,000 people were homeless and became refugees in the big towns.

King Paul succeeded to the throne in 1949. Constantine Karamanlis became Prime Minister in 1955. He resigned in 1963 after a dispute with King Paul. During this period many improvements were made in the war-battered economy of Greece, including the promotion of tourism.

King Constantine succeeded to the throne in 1963 and in 1964 George Papandreou was elected Prime Minister. There were many disputes between the King and Prime Minister over the control of the army.

On April 21, 1967 the army seized power under the leadership of Colonels Papadopoulos, Patakos and Makarezos. Martial law was proclaimed. In the same year King Constantine attempted a counter-revolution. This failed, and the king was obliged to leave the country.

These colonels were deposed by another army coup in November 1973. Only eight months later this régime fell after meddling in Cyprus and Karamanlis returned.

▲ October 28 is celebrated annually by the Greeks to commemorate the war against Italy under Mussolini in 1940. The Greeks fought bravely, but were eventually defeated as a result of Germany's intervention.

▶ After the Germans advanced in 1941, life became difficult. Arrests and daily executions were used to control resistance. Some 350,000 Greeks died, by execution, in enemy hands, in armed clashes, or from lack of food.

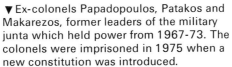

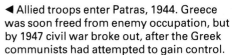
◄ Allied troops enter Patras, 1944. Greece was soon freed from enemy occupation, but by 1947 civil war broke out, after the Greek communists had attempted to gain control.

▼ Constantine became king in 1964, but was forced into exile in 1967. In 1973 he was deposed. A referendum on the future of the monarchy was held in 1974. 69% of the people voted to abolish the monarchy.

▼ Ex-colonels Papadopoulos, Patakos and Makarezos, former leaders of the military junta which held power from 1967-73. The colonels were imprisoned in 1975 when a new constitution was introduced.

Myths and heroes

Gods and heroes

The ancient Greeks first used myths to explain the mysteries of nature. Their gods looked and behaved much like humans. They were not mortal beings but represented physical forces. The greatest gods were the Olympians—twelve deities ruled by Zeus, king of the Gods.

Rhapsodists, the greatest of whom was Homer, moved from one princely court to another and sang the glorious deeds of Achaean rulers. The *Iliad* and *Odyssey* are attributed to Homer. The last phase of the siege of Troy forms the subject of the *Iliad*. Achilles and Agamemnon, King of Mycenae are the heroes. In the *Odyssey*, Odysseus King of Ithica is the hero, and the epic concerns his wanderings after the fall of Troy. Classical Greece based its entire educational effort on a thorough teaching of these two epic poems.

A similar attitude to folk worship continued during the Byzantine civilization. Patron saints, such as St. Demetrius of Byzantium and modern Thessaloniki took the place of gods such as Athena in classical Athens.

As in classical times, people of great achievements are much admired in Modern Greece. Modern heroes include such people as the late Aristotle Onassis for his achievements in shipping and finance.

▼ Jason was a mythical hero sent to fetch the golden fleece, which hung on an oak tree in a grove, guarded by a dragon. Many famous heroes sailed with him in his ship Argos. They became known as the Argonauts. Medea, who fell in love with Jason, touched the dragon's eyelids with magic ointment and it went to sleep, allowing Jason to steal the fleece.

◄ Theseus, son of King Aegeus of Athens, went to Crete as one of fourteen sent each year to the Minotaur, a dreadful monster in a labyrinth at Knossos. Theseus killed the Minotaur, and his escape was aided by the ball of string which Ariadne had given him to guide him to safety. On returning to Athens, Theseus forgot to substitute a white sail for the black one flown in the ships that carried the victims to Crete. Aegeus, who thought his son was dead, drowned himself in the Aegean Sea, which takes its name from him.

▼ After the war with Troy, Odysseus took ten years to return to his kingdom, Ithaca. His many adventures are recounted by Homer in the *Odyssey*. One of his adventures concerns the beautiful Sirens who sat on the shore and sang so sweetly that men who heard them could not resist them, and were lured onto the rocks. Odysseus passed safely by blocking his men's ears with wax. He was tied to a mast so that he could hear the Sirens without danger.

▲ Karagiozis is a Greek folk character portrayed in shadow theatre. The action usually takes place in a country under Turkish rule. Karagiozis is a hunchback with a huge nose and an abnormally long arm. He is cunning, lazy and an incorrigible liar. He often appears with his sons.

▲ Onassis, who died in 1975 aged 69, was the most famous of Greek shipowners.

◄ Zorba is a fictional character devised by Nicos Kazantzakis. Zorba, as interpreted by Anthony Quinn in the film version, became the foreigner's image of a Greek.

The Greek character

Pride in achievement

Greeks try to be courteous and dignified. They can be chivalrous, helpful, generous and hospitable, and take pride in what they do.

Greeks also try to avoid unpleasantness. When it seems that a situation is becoming difficult, and tempers will be lost, they will wait, and talk it over. Given a job to do, Greeks like to prove that they can do things quickly, cheaply and efficiently, but they are always on the watch in case they are being tricked. This shrewdness can have a sharper side! Some Greeks are also proud and quick to take offence — perhaps because success in their work matters a great deal, and it is wounding to appear silly.

Greek attitudes

Many Greeks dislike rudeness. If someone is in the way in a public place, they may be nudged to one side — not aggressively, but rather impersonally, as if someone were moving a chair out of the way. Chivalry is not extended to the ill-mannered.

Greeks far prefer to live among crowds. Even farmworkers will live in a packed village and walk out to work every day, so that evenings can be spent talking. This can often mean argument, sometimes the banging of fists and shouting. Greek people are interested in the complexities of issues, and like to discuss them in great detail. Finding a conclusion tends to seem an anti-climax. Many Greeks see power as corrupting, and so can be very critical when discussing governments and political systems. This may be because the Greeks almost invented politics!

▲ The Greeks believe in being chivalrous. They are particularly courteous to older people and always ready to help them in public places.

▲ Generally, Greeks hate being alone. At times they would rather be with someone they dislike than be alone.

▲ The Greeks like to think they are helpful, generous and hospitable. Very often, a youth, or an elderly villager will drop whatever he is doing to help a tourist out of trouble.

▲ Greeks are ready to argue about anything, especially about football and politics. Although they may shout and wave their arms about, they calm down quickly.

▲ The Greeks are often thought to be quick on the uptake. This can make them seem a little suspicious, even to one another: Greeks do not like to be tricked.

▲ Concepts of time differ among cultures. Although Greeks will make appointments they do not become anxious if it seems they may be late.

▲ Due to rapid, uneven changes in society, new and old attitudes to life constantly meet each other in Greece.

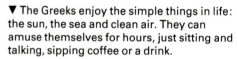

▼ The Greeks enjoy the simple things in life: the sun, the sea and clean air. They can amuse themselves for hours, just sitting and talking, sipping coffee or a drink.

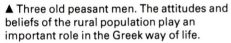

▲ Three old peasant men. The attitudes and beliefs of the rural population play an important role in the Greek way of life.

▲ Since the War of Independence, Greeks have been trying to acquire the confidence to come to terms with a great past which is admired by all the world.

How Greece is changing

Recovery from war

After World War II Greece was a hungry and depressed country, involved in a terrible civil war. Since then, the Greeks have worked hard turning their country into a prosperous and busy place, with traffic chaos and parking problems.

The pattern of living in flats within large towns is increasing. Well-built houses in the suburbs are rapidly knocked down and replaced by apartment blocks. In recent years, some 10 per cent of the Athens area has been under construction at any time.

Of course the Western world is better off than it was in 1949, and Greece prospered when the drachma was devalued in 1953 and the country became really cheap for foreign tourists. More and more people came and hotels and roads were built rapidly. More and more taxis, cars for hire, ships and ferry boats became necessary in all parts of Greece.

A growing prosperity

Since the war the emphasis has been on planned use of the country's natural resources. Assistance was given to unify agricultural holdings. Land improvement programmes were undertaken. Dams have been erected to ensure adequate irrigation.

The European Economic Community

The Treaty of Accession to the EEC, which was signed in May 1979, made Greece the tenth member of the Community or Common Market on January 1981. Membership will stimulate the growth of agriculture and industry.

Greece's agriculture, which relies heavily on the export of crops such as olives, citrus fruits and grapes, will be subsidized, and farmers' incomes will be supplemented from EEC funds. Industry will also be subsidized. Over a five-year transitional period, Greece will adopt the Community's international trading policies.

Trends in modern Greece

▲ From 1955, when Constantine Karamanlis became Prime Minister, Greece started on the road to prosperity, with traffic chaos and parking problems. Houses are replaced by apartment blocks with modern amenities. Tourism has become a major source of foreign exchange, and now oil has been discovered.

▲ Life in rural areas is often primitive. This woman is raising water from a deep well, and will have to carry it home. Many younger workers are leaving the countryside, and agriculture suffers as a result.

▼ The impact of tourism is changing the Greek coastlines. Large sums of money are spent on the construction of beach installations along the coastline. Organized beach facilities are equipped with changing rooms, showers, restaurants and snack bars and deck chairs.

▲ Workmen on an apartment block. To keep up with the demand for more housing, sound, individual houses are rapidly replaced by apartment blocks. In recent years, as much as 10 per cent of all the Athens area has been under construction at one time.

▲ In November 1973 the army stepped in to crush student demonstrations. On November 25th, 1973, the army led a second coup ousting Papadopoulos. General Gizikis was sworn in as President.

▼ Delighted crowds welcome the return of civilian government to Greece in July 1974. The military government was forced to resign after mishandling the Cyprus situation and recalled Karamanlis, a former premier.

Reference
Human and physical geography

The climate of Greece

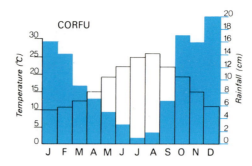
CORFU

Greece has a Mediterranean type of climate. Most rain falls in the winter; summers are hot and dry. Macedonia, on the leeward slopes of the Pindus mountains, is the least well-watered, parts receiving less than 50cm. of rain a year. This climate, and the rugged landscape combine to make Greece an arid country, best suited to succulent vegetation able to withstand high evaporation during the hot summer.

Apart from the northern mountains, Greece averages well over 300 sunny days each year. July temperatures average around 25°C (77°F) and January around 5°C (40°F). It is much colder in the mountains, which frequently experience winter snow. Island temperatures are more equable, cooled by sea breezes in summer.

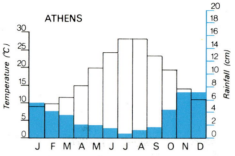
ATHENS

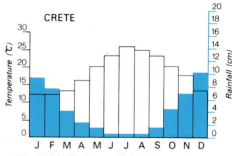
CRETE

Natural vegetation in Greece

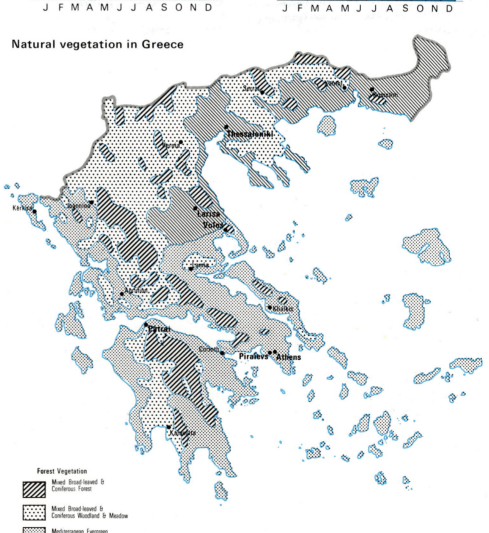

Forest Vegetation

- Mixed Broad-leaved & Coniferous Forest
- Mixed Broad-leaved & Coniferous Woodland & Meadow
- Mediterranean Evergreen Maquis & Meadow
- Submediterranean Oaks & Pines

The population density

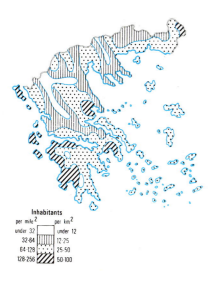

Inhabitants
per mile²	per km²
under 32	under 12
32-64	12-25
64-128	25-50
128-256	50-100

The population of Greece in 1980 was 9,500,000 with an overall density of 70 inhabitants per square kilometre. The distribution of population is unequal, as in all mountainous countries. Greater Athens, for example, has 5,867 inhabitants per square kilometre. The island of Crete has 54.8 inhabitants per square kilometre and Thrace has 38.4 inhabitants per square kilometre.

Through the ages emigration has played an important role in the history of Greece. Many thousands of people have emigrated to America and other industrialized countries in the twentieth century, hoping to find good jobs and secure homes. The exodus continued until the early 1970s. But in 1974 returning emigrants exceeded the number leaving. With Greece's growing prosperity, this trend is likely to continue.

The populations of principal towns

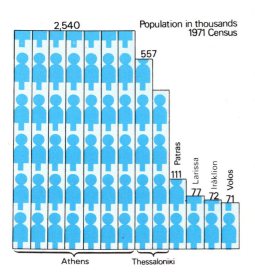

Population in thousands 1971 Census

2,540 — Athens
557 — Thessaloniki
111 — Patras
77 — Larissa
72 — Iráklion
71 — Volos

Government

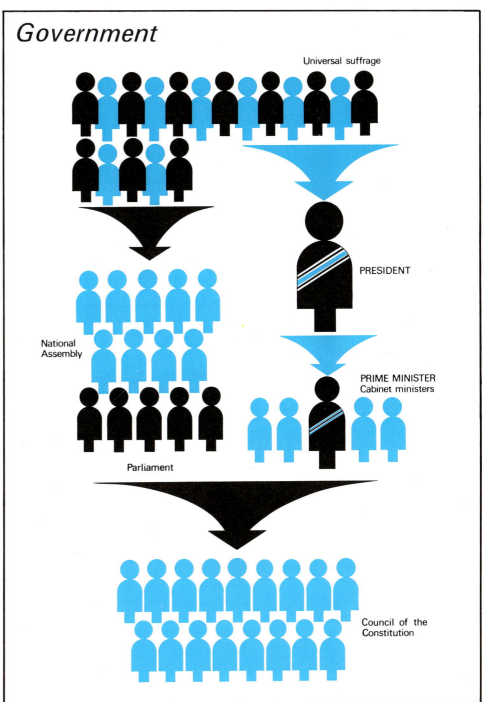

Universal suffrage

National Assembly

PRESIDENT

Parliament

PRIME MINISTER
Cabinet ministers

Council of the Constitution

The power of the Army

Greece has not had the opportunity to develop a stable tradition of democratic government in modern times. It has the unfortunate fate to be a small, poor country in a world conflict area. Eastern Mediterranean has experienced many violent upheavals in the twentieth century. Greece has, during this period, been a constitutional monarchy, a country invaded by foreign powers; it has experienced devastating civil war, and five army coups.

The colonels' coup of 1967 suspended parliamentary government, until a new constitution was drawn up in 1968. In May 1973 Greece was declared a republic and the monarchy abolished. Six months later another army coup replaced the 1967 regime

with a new group of officers. These officers resigned in July 1974, after a bungled attempt to play the power game, which brought the country to the brink of war with Turkey. The former Prime Minister returned, in an attempt to restore constitutional government.

The 1975 constitution is based on democratic principles. The Prime Minister and Ministers of departments oversee affairs of national importance. Many other essential functions are exercised by the seven regional authorities.

The regions are further divided into 52 provinces, called *Nomoi*. Each *Nomos* is in turn divided into municipalities called *Demoi*, and into communities. There are 256 *Demoi* and 5808 communities. The Minister of the Interior coordinates all regional activities.

Reference
History

MAIN EVENTS IN GREEK HISTORY

B.C.
3500 Evidence of late Neolithic man found in Crete.

GROWTH OF THE CITY STATE
2000 Palaces are built in Crete at Knossos and Phaestos, where the military rulers live. Cretan ships begin to visit the ports of Cyclades islands, Argolis, Egypt and the Adriatic Sea.
1700 The early palaces at Knossos, Phaestos and Malia are destroyed.
1600 Building activity is again at its height. Architectural tastes and artistic trends have developed further.
1580 The war chariot is imported into Greece.
1525-20 The second destruction of Cretan civilization takes place.
1450 Mycenaeans capture Knossos and their princes become rulers of the great Minoan city.
1300 Theseus unites the townships of Attica in a federation under the leadership of Athens.
1200 End of Late Minoan Civilization.
1194-84 Trojan War occurs and Troy is sacked and burned down.
1150 Late phase of Mycenaean Age.
c. 1000 The Dorians colonize the islands of Thera, Melos, Crete and Rhodes and cross into Asia Minor. Dorians also invade south east Peloponnese and later call themselves *Spartans*.
c. 950 Monarchical regimes begin to weaken and power passes to the aristocracy.
900-600 Sparta asserts her primacy in the Peloponnese.
776 First Olympic Games are held.
750-550 Great colonizing movements take place.

594 Dracon draws up a severe code of laws for Athens.
586-394 Pythian Games are held in honour of Apollo at Delphi.
550 Ionians are conquered by Cyrus the Great of Persia.
550-490 Ionians revolt against Persians and first invasion of Greek mainland by Persians takes place.
356-323 Alexander the Great.

A.D.
THE BYZANTINE EMPIRE
273 Constantine the Great becomes Emperor of Eastern Roman Empire.
330 Start of the Byzantine Empire.
527 Justinian becomes Emperor of Byzantium.
1204 Franks invade Greece.
1453 Byzantine Empire falls to the Ottoman Turks.

TURKISH RULE
1456 Omar, son of Turachon, captures Athens.
1456-1681 First phase of Turkish occupation of Greece.
1466 The Parthenon is converted into a mosque with a minaret.
1687 Count Morosini bombards the Acropolis from his ships. A shell from a mortar falls with disastrous results on the Parthenon which at that time is used as a powder magazine.
1775-95 The notoriously cruel Turkish governor Hadji Ali Hasseki rules Athens.
1814 The "Society of Friends" is formed and becomes a rallying point for all Greek patriots.
1821 War of Independence.
1824 Lord Byron is struck down with fever and dies at Missolongi.
1827 The Greeks and allied fleets of Britain, France and Russia destroy the Turkish navy at the Bay of Navarino.
1829 Mahmoud II, Sultan of the Ottoman Turks, brings the fighting to an end by conceding independence to the Greeks.

MODERN GREECE
1830 London Protocol is signed, making the Greek State an independent monarchy.
1862 Military revolt is followed by King Othon being deposed by the National Assembly.
1864-1911 Second constitution of Greece under King George I.
1912-13 Greece at war with Turkey.
1913 King George I, murdered in Salonika, is succeeded by Constantine I.
1920 King Constantine I is bitten by a monkey and dies of blood poisoning. He is succeeded by George II.
1922 Greek Army is defeated by Turks.
1923 King George II leaves Greece after a military coup by Colonel Plastiras.
1924 Greece is declared a republic and Admiral Condilis becomes provisional President.
1925 General Pangalos seizes power.
1935 King George II is recalled by plebiscite.
1936 General Metaxas proclaims martial law.
1940 Courageous defence by Greek Army against Mussolini's troops.
1944 Greece is liberated by Allied Forces and full scale communist revolt breaks out.
1946 First elections held for eleven years.
1947-9 Communists attempt another take-over and a full scale civil war erupts in Greece.
1952 Greece becomes a member of the Atlantic Alliance.
1964 King Paul is succeeded by his son Constantine.
1967 Military Revolution led by Colonels Papadopoulos, Macarezos and Patakos takes place and King Constantine's attempted counter-revolution fails.
1968 New Constitution is approved by plebiscite.
1973 The monarchy is abolished and Greece declared a Democratic Republic with George Papadopoulos as President. Later in the same year he is dismissed after students and workers uprising.
1974 Military government resigns over Cyprus situation. Constantinos Karamanlis recalled to form government. Referendum on monarchy. 69% vote for a Republic.
1975 The new Constitution is approved by Parliament on June 7th. Constantinos Tsatsos elected President. The leaders of the Junta are jailed.
1980 Constantinos Karamanlis elected President.
1981 Greece became 10th member of the EEC. Papandreou forms the first socialist government.
1982 Civil marriage is introduced. Church marriages are accepted on an equal footing. The system of dowry is abolished.

The Arts

CLASSICAL
DRAMA (FIFTH CENTURY B.C.)
Aeschylus (525-456 B.C.): introduced dialogue, curtailing the role of the chorus. His most important works were *Agamemnon; Eumenides; Choëphori; The Persians*

Sophocles (495-406 B.C.): increased the number of dramatic actors to three and the chorus to 15. His most famous works are *Ajax; Antigone; Oedipus at Colonus; Oedipus Rex*

Euripides (480-406 B.C.): wrote some 92 tragedies in all and his most famous are *Andromache; Electra; Hippolytus; Medea; Orestes*

Aristophanes (450-385 B.C.): satirized great men of his time. He wrote 40 comedies including *the Acharnians; the Clouds; the Frogs; Peace*

HISTORY (FIFTH CENTURY B.C.)
Herodotus (484-424 B.C.): has been called the "father of history", because he wrote systematically for the first time, concerning a period of 240 years

Thucydides (460-399 B.C.): the greatest historian of ancient Greece continued from where Herodotus left off and carried the story of Greek development to 411 B.C.

POETRY (NINTH CENTURY B.C. AND LATER)
Homer (ninth century B.C.): wrote the *Iliad* and *Odyssey*, the world's greatest epic poems

Hesiod (eighth century B.C.): wrote poems about the gods and nature

Sappho (610-565 B.C.): greatest of the lyric poets

Pindar (518-446 B.C.): wrote odes, called Pindaric odes

Philosophy (fifth century B.C.)
Socrates (470-399 B.C.): changed the current of human thought, without writing a word, simply by talking in the streets of Athens. He was committed to trial for impiety and sentenced to death

ARCHITECTURE AND SCULPTURE (FIFTH CENTURY B.C.)
Myron (fifth century) sculptor, works include *the Bronze Bull* and *the Discus Thrower*

Polycleitus (fifth century): famous for his *Doryphoros* and *the Statue of an Athlete*

Phidias (480-431 B.C.): was the greatest of sculptors. He created *the statue of the Athena Parthenos,* housed inside the Parthenon; he also did the pediments and the frieze of the Parthenon

Ictinus and Calicrates architects for the Parthenon, the most perfect of all buildings. It was built between 447-437 B.C.

PHILOSOPHY (FOURTH CENTURY B.C.)
Plato (427-347 B.C.) became Socrates' pupil and his most effective spokesman. His works include the *Laws;* the *Critics;* the *Republic;* the *Symposium;* the *Apology* and *Gorgias.*

Aristotle (384-322 B.C.) whose most famous works include *Ethics* and *Politics,* became Plato's pupil in 368 B.C. He later became Alexander the Great's tutor.

Xenophon (430-355 B.C.) also a pupil of Socrates became a historian and philosopher and wrote such important works as *the Anabasis* (the Retreat); *Memorabilia; Economics.*

ARCHITECTURE AND SCULPTURE (FOURTH CENTURY B.C.)
Polycletus the younger built the sanctuary at Epidaurus, between 350-330 B.C.

Praxitelis was the outstanding sculptor of the fourth century B.C. and his greatest work was the statue of the God Hermes, dated 350-340 B.C.

Apellos was a painter in the court of Alexander the Great and his most famous work was *Aphrodite Anadyomene*, a painting dedicated to the Asklepieion on the island of Cos.

THE OLYMPIAN PANTHEON
Of the twenty supreme gods only twelve were admitted into the grand council:

Zeus the ruling power of air or sky and supreme god of the pagan Greek world. He was the head of the most powerful celestial dynasty. Zeus sent the rain and lightning

Hera the wife of Zeus and queen of heaven

Poseidon brother of Zeus and god of the sea

Hestia sister of Zeus and goddess of fire

Demeter sister of Zeus and goddess of agriculture

Apollo son of Zeus and Hera, god of day, music and poetry

Artemis daughter of Zeus and Hera, goddess of hunting and chastity

Hermes son of Zeus and Hera, god of eloquence, messenger of the gods

Athena daughter of Zeus (born from his head), goddess of wisdom, who gave her name to the city of Athens. The owl, an emblem frequently seen, was sacred to Athena

Ares son of Zeus and Hera, god of war and tumult

Hephaestus crippled son of Zeus and Hera, god of fire, trained as a blacksmith by Poseidon

Aphrodite born of the foam of the sea and was goddess of love and beauty (Eros was her son).

POST-CLASSICAL ART AND ARCHITECTURE
El Greco (Dominicos Theotocopoulos) sixteenth century painter, settled in Spain.

Lytras, Nikiforos nineteenth century painter from the island of Tinos.

Volomakis, Constantine from the island of Crete, painted seascapes at the time of the War of Independence.

Isaias, Alexander painted scenes from the War of Independence.

Tsokos, Dimitrios portrait painter.

Gzis, Nikolaos nineteenth century painter—considered one of the greatest Greek artists. He was from the island of Tinos.

Tsarouhis modern painter and stage designer.

Kleanthis, Stamatis (1802-62) architect of the first Athens University building.

MUSIC
Skalkoltas, Nikos (1904-49) distinguished exponent of atonal music. Used Greek folk music in his work.

Hadjidakis, Manos (1921-) raised the "bouzoukia" (urban folk music) to an artistic level. Works include *Six Folk Pictures,* music for the film *Never on Sunday.*

Theodorakis, Mikis (1925-) internationally known composer; works include *Epitaphios; March of the Spirit*

LITERATURE
Kornaros, Vitsentzos poet who lived during the Turkish Occupation.

Korais, Adamantios (1748-1833) a scholar who played an important part in the cultural and national revival of Greece prior to the War of Independence.

Hristopoulos, Athanasios (1772-1847) composed graceful and attractive poetry.

Solomos, Dionysius (1798-1857) composed the *Hymn to Liberty*—a song devoted to the War of Independence, which subsequently was set to music and became the national anthem. Other important poems include *the Free Besieged; Lambros;* and *Kriticos*

Valaoritis, Aristotelis a poet of the Ionian Islands School, whose work commemorates the heroes of the War of Independence and includes *Mnimosyna; Athanasios Diakos; Kyra Frosyni: Foteinos.*

Palamas, Kostis (1859-1943) who wrote poems such as *Dodeklogoston Gyfton* and *the King's Flute*

Xenopoulos, Gregoris playwright of the late nineteenth century

Carafy, Constantine (1863-1933) poet of international fame—known as the "Poet of Alexandria" as he never lived in Greece.

Kazantzakis, Nikos (1883-1957) author of *Zorba the Greek* and *Christ Recrucified*

Seferis, Georgios (1900-1971) modern poet, winner of the 1963 Nobel Prize. Works include *King of Asine*

Ritsos, Yannis (1909-   ) poetry of political nature. Works include *Epìtaphiòs.*

Venezis, Elias (1904-1973) lyrical prose writer whose works include *Aeolia.*

Odysseus Elytis (1912-   ) wins Nobel Prize for Literature in 1979. Works include: *Axion Esti; The Mad Pomegranate Tree.*

Reference
The Economy

FACTS AND FIGURES

Total wealth produced: (1978)
US $32 billion

Wealth per head: US $3,440

Economic growth: (1979)
3.5 per cent

Main sources of income:
Agriculture: Tobacco, wheat, rye, barley, rice, cotton, olives, citrus fruits, raisins and figs. Sheep are the most important livestock.

Mining: Nickel, bauxite, iron ore, manganese, chrome, lead, zinc. Hydro-electric power and oil resources are beginning to be exploited.

Industry: Textiles, chemicals, food processing, aluminium, cement, glass, metallurgy, shipbuilding, domestic electrical equipment, footwear, handicrafts. Shipping and tourism are large earners of currency.

Main trading partners: Germany, Italy, France, United Kingdom, U.S.A., Saudi Arabia

Currency: 1 drachma = 100 lepta
£1 = 140 drachmes (January 1984)

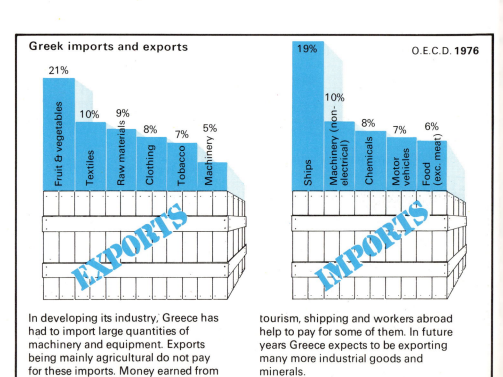

Cattle
Pigs
Sheep
Principal Fishing Ports
Oats
Wheat
Rice
Cotton
Sugar Beet
Potatoes
Grapes
Maize
Olives
Tobacco
Apples
Citrus Fruit

Greece is still largely an agricultural country, though in recent years there has been a determined effort to industrialize. The second World War and the subsequent civil war had left industry and agriculture in ruins. Since then the major effort of development has gone into industry. Agriculture was, and is, old-fashioned in its methods. Farms are small, modern equipment scarce and the land is in need of irrigation. Many people are tending to leave the country and seek a better pay in the towns.

Government policies have encouraged highly mechanized industries e.g. steel, chemicals, fertilizers and food processing. Much needed foreign currency (to pay for imports) is being attracted in many ways—tourism, shipping and the remittances of workers abroad being the most important. Foreign companies have also been encouraged to set up factories in Greece.

A barrier to industrial progress is the shortage of managers and of businessmen capable of exploiting opportunities on a large scale. The Greek economy is however expanding and despite high inflation there is every indication that it will continue to do so.

Greek imports and exports   O.E.C.D. **1976**

EXPORTS:
21% Fruit & vegetables
10% Textiles
9% Raw materials
8% Clothing
7% Tobacco
5% Machinery

IMPORTS:
19% Ships
10% Machinery (non-electrical)
8% Chemicals
7% Motor vehicles
6% Food (exc. meat)

In developing its industry, Greece has had to import large quantities of machinery and equipment. Exports being mainly agricultural do not pay for these imports. Money earned from tourism, shipping and workers abroad help to pay for some of them. In future years Greece expects to be exporting many more industrial goods and minerals.

58

How labour is employed

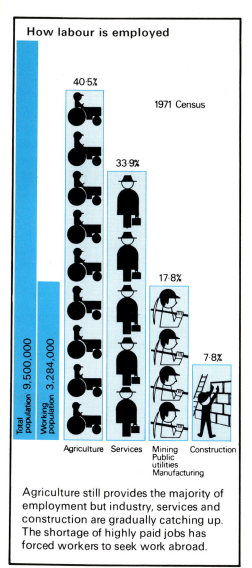

40.5%
33.9%
17.8%
7.8%

1971 Census

Total population 9,500,000
Working population 3,284,000

Agriculture | Services | Mining Public utilities Manufacturing | Construction

Agriculture still provides the majority of employment but industry, services and construction are gradually catching up. The shortage of highly paid jobs has forced workers to seek work abroad.

Industry in Greece

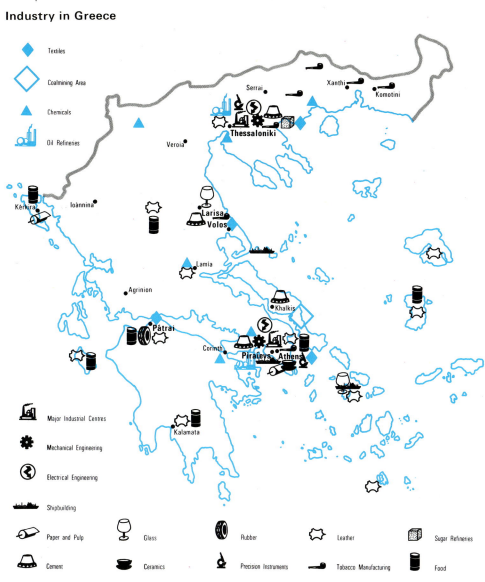

Textiles

Coalmining Area

Chemicals

Oil Refineries

Serrai · Xanthi · Komotini
Thessaloniki
Veroia
Kérkira · Ioánnina
Larisa · Volos
Lamia
Agrinion
Khalkis
Pátrai
Corinth · Piraievs · Athens
Kalamata

Major Industrial Centres

Mechanical Engineering

Electrical Engineering

Shipbuilding

Paper and Pulp | Glass | Rubber | Leather | Sugar Refineries

Cement | Ceramics | Precision Instruments | Tobacco Manufacturing | Food

What is owned compared with other countries

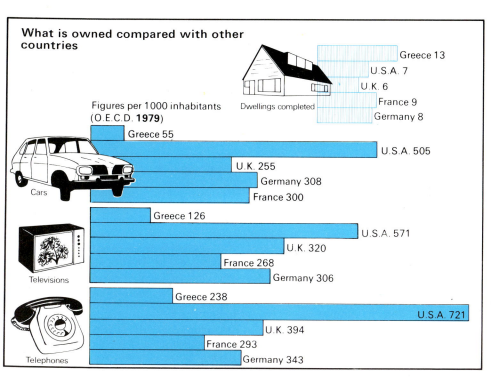

Figures per 1000 inhabitants (O.E.C.D. 1979)

Dwellings completed
Greece 13
U.S.A. 7
U.K. 6
France 9
Germany 8

Cars
Greece 55
U.S.A. 505
U.K. 255
Germany 308
France 300

Televisions
Greece 126
U.S.A. 571
U.K. 320
France 268
Germany 306

Telephones
Greece 238
U.S.A. 721
U.K. 394
France 293
Germany 343

The rise in prices and incomes

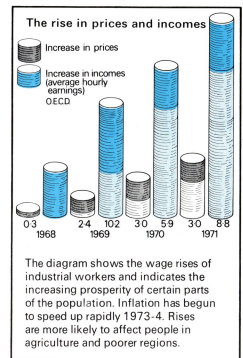

Increase in prices

Increase in incomes (average hourly earnings) O.E.C.D.

0·3 | 2·4 10·2 | 3·0 5·9 | 3·0 8·8
1968 | 1969 | 1970 | 1971

The diagram shows the wage rises of industrial workers and indicates the increasing prosperity of certain parts of the population. Inflation has begun to speed up rapidly 1973-4. Rises are more likely to affect people in agriculture and poorer regions.

Gazetteer

Aegean Sea. Arm of the Mediterranean between Greece and Turkey. Dotted with islands, mostly belonging to Greece: i.e. the Dodecanese, the Cyclades, the N. Sporades and Euboea.

Alexandroupolís. (40 50N 25 55E) Capital of the Evros *nomos* in Thrace. Pop. 18,712.

Athens. (37 59N 23 42E) Athena in Greek. Capital of Greece and largest city. Pop. 2,540,000. Economic and cultural centre of Greece. Named after its patron goddess, Athena. In 5th century B.C. became leading Greek city state and beat the Persians with its powerful navy. During this time, known as the Golden Age, art and literature flourished. Defeated by Sparta in Peloponnesian war 431-404 B.C. Conquered by Romans 86 B.C. By the time of the War of Independence (1834) the town had declined to a population of 5,000, but afterwards it grew very rapidly. Manufactures textiles, rugs, chemicals, wine, etc. Centre for tourism, government, education

Canea. (35 20N 20 24E) Khania in Greek. Capital of Crete. Sea-port. Badly damaged during the German invasion, 1941. Pop. 38,268.

Corfu. (39 30N 19 50E) Kerkira in Greek. Second largest and most beautiful of Ionian islands. Area 395 square km. (246 sq. miles). Mountains in north. Produces olive oil, wine, citrus fruits. Tourist centre. Under Venetian rule 1386-1797 and British from 1815-64, when ceded to Greece.

Corinth. (37 40N 22 58E) Korinthos in Greek. Port on Gulf of Corinth near end of Corinth Canal. Old Corinth, 5 km. (3 miles) S.W., was one of the most powerful ancient Greek cities. Destroyed by earthquake 1928. Pop. 15,892.

Corinth Canal. Ship canal 6.4 km. (4 miles) long, built 1881-93, cutting the Isthmus of Corinth, thus joining the Gulf of Corinth with the Saronic Gulf.

Crete. (35 15N 25 0E) Kriti in Greek. Fourth largest island in Mediterranean. Area 5,177 sq. km. (3,217 sq. miles). Capital Canea. Mostly mountainous. Mt. Idha, 2,438 m. (8,000 ft.), highest peak. Main products are olive oil, citrus fruit, wine. Home of Minoan civilization, begun c. 3400 B.C. Palace of Knossos has revealed the richness of Minoan culture. Pop. 483,258.

Cyclades. (37 30N 25 15E) Group of over 200 islands in Aegean Sea. Includes, Paros Naxos, Andros, Delos, Mikonos, Tinos, Ios, Kithnos. Capital Hermoupolis on Syros. Produce wine, tobacco, olives, minerals. Ruled by Turkey from 16th century; passed to Greece in 1832.

Delphi. (38 30N 22 40E) Ancient city and seat of famous oracle at foot of Parnassus mountains. Pythian Games held here every four years from 582 B.C.

Dodecanese. (36 40N 27 0E) Group of islands in S.E. Aegean Sea, including Rhodes and Kos. Capital Rhodes. Passed to Greece in 1947.

Epirus. (39 50N 20 20E) Region between Pindus Mountains and Ionian Sea. Mountainous and not very fertile. Famous for horses and cattle.

Euboea. (38 30N 23 50E) Largest Aegean island. Capital Chalcis. Largely mountainous. Produces cereals, vines, olives, sheep and goats. Linked to mainland by road bridge.

Ionian Islands. (38 40N 20 0E) Group of islands in Ionian Sea including Corfu, Levkás, Kefallinía and Zakinthos.

Iráklion. (35 20N 25 10E) Largest city of Crete. Sea-port with large coastal trade. Exports olive oil, wine, raisins. Manufactures soap, leather, wine. Ancient Minoan port. Pop. 77,000.

Kalamata. (37 2N 22 7E) Capital of Messenia *nomos* in S.W. Pelopennese. Port. Exports citrus fruit, olives. Manufactures cigarettes.

Katerini. (40 15N 22 30E) Capital of Pieria *nomos*. Agricultural centre. Pop. 28,824.

Kaválla. (41 0N 24 4E) Capital of Kaválla *nomos*. Port. Exports tobacco. Pop. 44,406.

Kefallinía. (38 15N 20 33E) Largest of Ionian Islands. Pop. 46,302. Mountainous. Mainly agricultural. Devastated by earthquake 1953.

Komotíni. (41 6N 25 32E) Capital of Rodhopi *nomos* in Thrace. Market town. Pop. 29,734.

Kos. (36 40N 27 10E) Island in Aegean Sea in Dodecanese. Low-lying and fertile. Produces cereals, olives, fruits and wine. Ancient library and medical centre. Birth place of Hippocrates.

Lamía. (38 45N 22 30E) Capital of Phthiotis *nomos*. Market town. Pop. 22,353.

Larisa. (39 38N 22 26E) Capital of Larisa *nomos*. Agriculture and trade. Railway junction. Manufactures textiles. Pop. 72,000.

Lesvos. (39 10N 26 34E) Island in Aegean Sea off Turkish coast. Pop. 117,000. Fertile lowlands produce wheat, olives, fruits and wine. Chief town Mitilini.

Levkás. (38 40N 20 35E) One of Ionian Islands. Chief products olive oil and wine. Pop. 28,969.

Limnos. (39 50N 25 10E) Island in Aegean Sea. Pop. 22,000. Mountainous. Chief town Kastron.

Macedonia. (40 45N 23 0E) Division of N. Greece. Pop. 1,890,654.

Missolongi. (38 25N 21 25E) Capital of *nomos* of Aetolia and Acarnania. Agriculture. Famous for its defence against Turks in 1822-6. Byron died here in 1824. Pop. 11,266.

Mycenae. (37·45N 22 45E) Ancient city in N.E. Peloponnese. Flourished in 1400 B.C. Destroyed in fifth century B.C.

Navplia. (37 30N 22 50E) Capital of Argolis *nomos*. Seaport trading in tobacco, fruit and vegetables. Capital of Greece 1822-34. Pop 8.918.

Naxos. (37 5N 25 29E) Largest island in Cyclades. Produces wine, fruit, olives, emery. Pop. 19,000.

Olympia. (37 40N 21 39E) Ancient city. Site of ruined temple of Zeus. Founded c. 1000 B.C. Olympic Games held here from 776 B.C. Tourist centre.

Olympus. (37 40N 21 39E) Mountain 2,917 m. (9,570 feet) high; Greece's highest mountain. Traditional home of the gods.

Parnassus. (38 20N 22 30E) Mountain 2,457 m. (8,061 feet) high. Sacred mountain of ancient Greece.

Patras. (38 15N 21 47E) Capital of Achaea *nomos*. Seaport exporting currants, wine, olive oil, tobacco. Manufactures textiles. Pop. 111,000.

Peloponnese. (37 50N 22 0E) Peninsula in S. Greece joined to mainland by Isthmus of Corinth. Largely mountainous. Produces vines, citrus fruits and olives. Pop. 1,092,822.

Pindus Mountains. (39 30N 21 30E) Range about 100 miles long between Epirus and Thessaly.

Piraeus. (37 57N 23 30E) Seaport 8 km. (5 miles) S.W. of Athens. Leading Greek port and industrial centre. Exports wine, olives. Occupations ship building, oil refining, flour milling. Manufactures fertilizers, textiles. Pop. 813,957.

Rhodes. (36 21N 28 17E) In Greek Ródhos. Largest island in the Dodecanese. Pop. 59,000. 16 km. from Turkish coast. Fertile land produces cereals, fruits, wine. Rhodes town manufactures cigarettes, brandy, etc. Founded 408 B.C. Taken by Knights of St. John in 1309, Turks 1523 and by Italy 1912. Ceded to Greece 1946.

Samos. (37 41N 26 50E) Island in Aegean Sea. Two miles from Turkey. Pop. 52,034. Capital Samos. Largely mountainous but fertile. Produces wine, olives, tobacco and fruit.

Serrai. (41 0N 23 30E) Capital of *nomos*. Pop. 40,063. Commercial centre manufacturing cigarettes and cotton goods.

Sporades. (39 20N 24 0E) Scattered islands of Aegean Sea divided into two groups— N. Sporades including Skíathos, Skopelos, Skiros, and S. Sporades known as Dodecanese.

Thasos. (40 40N 24 40E) Island in N. Aegean. Pop. 15,000. Produces wine and olive oil. Once famous for gold mines.

Thessaloníki. (40 38N 23 0E) Capital of Macedonia and *nomos*. Pop. 557,000. Seaport and second city of Greece. Industrial centre which manufactures textiles, metal goods, chemicals, cigarettes, etc. Railway and airline centre.

Thíra. (36 24N 25 26E) Island in Cyclades. Formerly known as Santorini. Pop. 10,000.

Thrace. (41 27N 26 30E) Region in N.E. Chief town Komotini. Produces tobacco, wheat, cotton. Pop. 356,708.

Vardar River. (41 30N 22 20E) Chief river of Macedonia rising in Yugoslavia and reaching Aegean Sea near Thessaloníki.

Volos. (39 26N 22 57E) Capital of Magnesia *nomos*. Chief port of Thessaly. Manufactures textiles, chemicals, cement. Pop. 71,000.

Xanthi. (41 5N 24 55E) Capital of *nomos*. Important trade in tobacco. Pop. 26,377.

Yannina. (39 40N 20 52E) Capital of *nomos*. Trade in cereals, wine and fruit. Pop. 34,997.

Zakinthos. (37 48N 20 57E) Most southerly of Ionian Islands. Capital of *nomos*. Produces cereals, wine and olive oil. Suffers from earthquakes.

Index

Numbers in **heavy** type refer to illustrations.